SECOND EDITION

Workbook

0

SUPER MINDS

Herbert Puchta · Peter Lewis-Jones

CAMBRIDGE
UNIVERSITY PRESS

Contents

Say Hello!

1  🎧 01 **Listen and say the names. Color.**

1 Match and say.

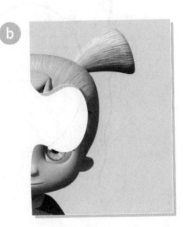

2 🎧 02 Listen and match.

1  **Listen and color.**

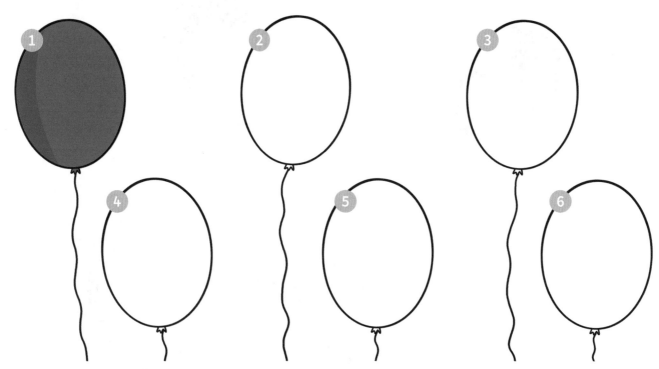

2 **Match and say.**

1 2 3 4 5 6

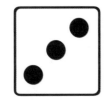 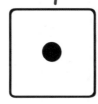 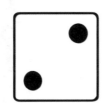   

1 🎧 **04** **Listen and point. Say the numbers.**

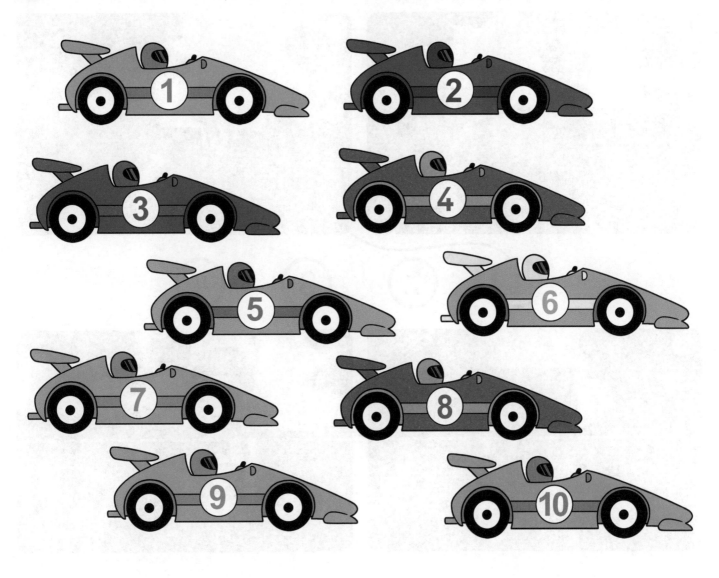

2 **Point and say. Count.**

1, 2, 3

1 🎧 **05** Listen and match.

2 🎧 **06** Listen and point.

1 What's good? Draw 😊.

2 Complete the picture. Draw yourself making friends.

1 🎧07 **Listen and match. Say.**

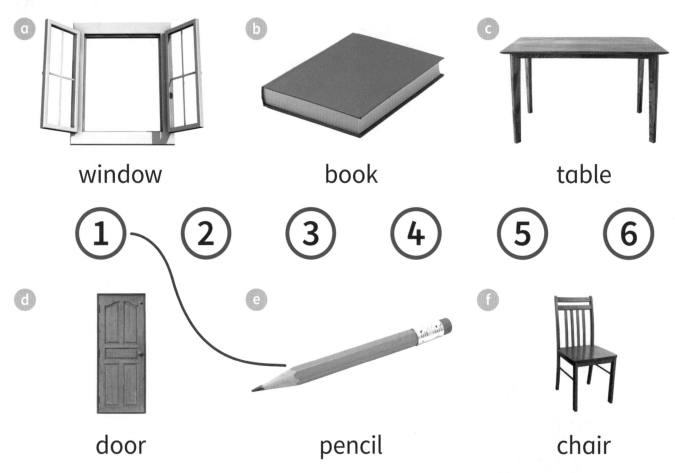

a window   **b** book   **c** table

① ② ③ ④ ⑤ ⑥

d door   **e** pencil   **f** chair

2 🎧08 **Listen and color.**

1 🎧 09 Listen and color.

2 🎧 10 Listen. Point and say.

sit down

1 🎧11 Listen. Point and sing.

2 🛡 Draw yourself in your classroom. Point and say.

1 🎧 12 Listen and circle.

1 ⓐ ⓑ

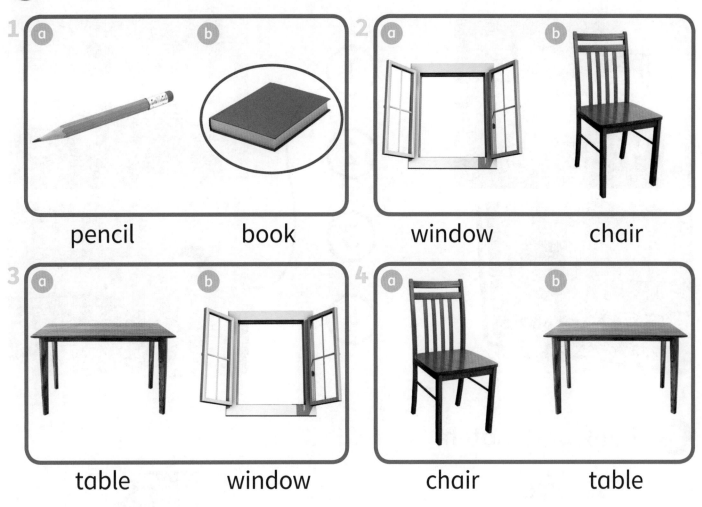

pencil   book

2 ⓐ ⓑ

window   chair

3 ⓐ ⓑ

table   window

4 ⓐ ⓑ

chair   table

2 🎧 13 Listen and point. Say.

What is it?

It's a pencil.

What is it? It's a (book). (13)

1 🎧 14 Listen and match.

2 Look and match.

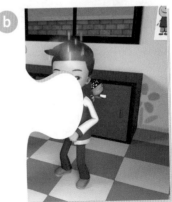

1 What's good? Draw 😊.

2 Look and find your favorite picture. Draw 😊.

My favorite is ...

1 🎧 **15** Listen and color.

①
②
③

2 Point and say the numbers.

| 1 | ? | 3 | ? | 5 | ? | 7 | ? | 9 | ? |

3 🛡 Look and say what's next.

①  **?**

② **?**

4 🛡 Find the wrong picture. X it out.

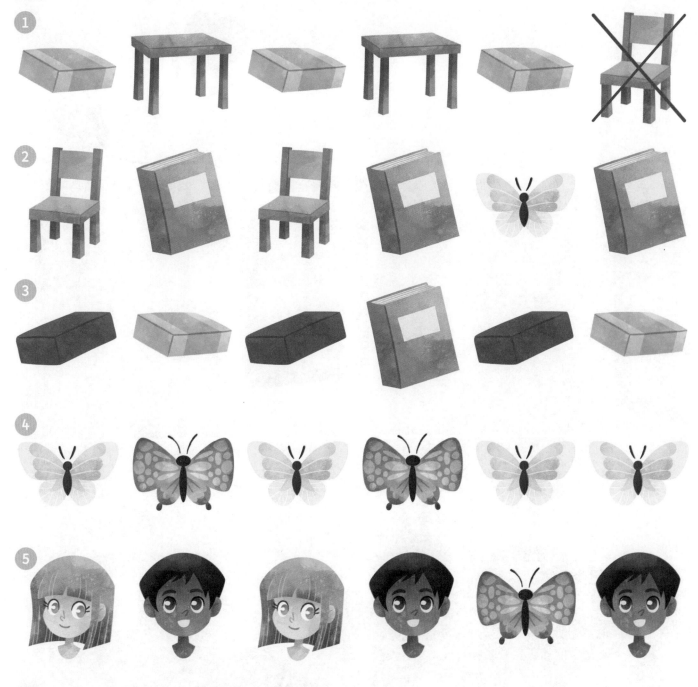

5 Complete the pattern. Say.

1 **Where does the butterfly go? Listen and draw.**

1 Look and say. Circle 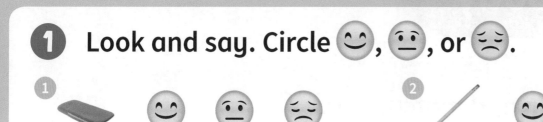.

1

2

3

4

2 What's in your classroom? Circle ☑ or ☒.

 BIG QUESTION What's in my classroom?

1  ☑ ☒
2 ☑ ☒
3  ☑ ☒
4 ☑ ☒

3 Color the objects.

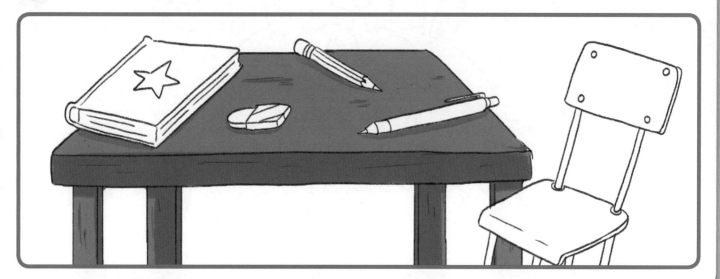

2 My Body

1 🎧 **17** Listen and match. Say.

2 🎧 **18** Listen and color.

1 🎧 19 **Listen to the monsters. Match.**

2 🛡 **Point. What does the monster say?**

I have 2 noses.

I have ...

1   **Listen. Trace and color.**

2 **Look and match. Color.**

 1

 2

 a

 b

1 🎧 21 **Listen to the monster. Circle ☑ or ☒.**

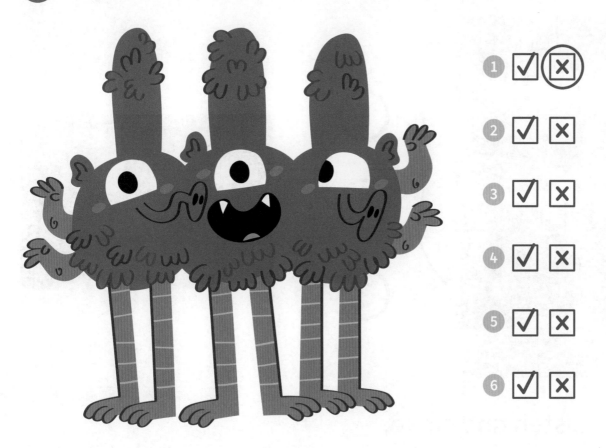

1 ☑ ⊗
2 ☑ ☒
3 ☑ ☒
4 ☑ ☒
5 ☑ ☒
6 ☑ ☒

2 **Look and remember. Cover. Ask and answer.**

What is it?

It's a nose!

1 🎧 22 Listen and match.

① ② ③

2 🎧 23 Listen and circle.

4

5

1 🛡️ What's good? Draw 😊.

2 🛡️ Look and circle 😊 or 😞.

1 🎧24 Listen and match. Say.

a run

b wave

c stand

① ② ③ ④ ⑤

d walk

e sit

2 🎧25 Listen and circle ☑ or ☒.

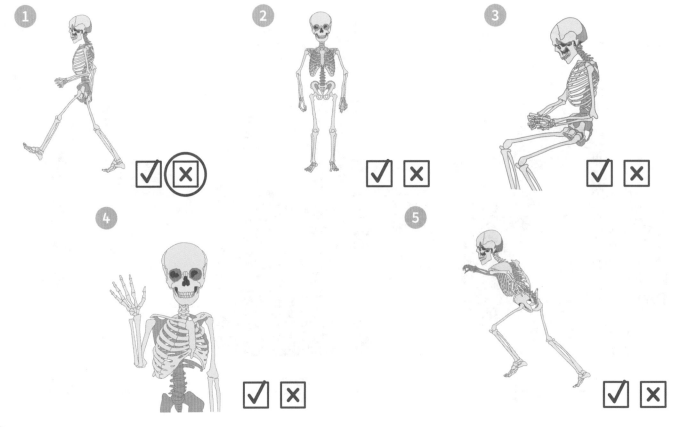

1 ☑ ⊗

2 ☑ ☒

3 ☑ ☒

4 ☑ ☒

5 ☑ ☒

3  **Listen and color.**

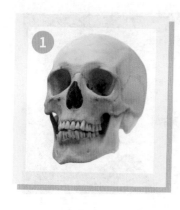

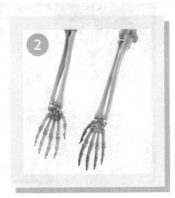

4 🎧 27 **Listen and match.**

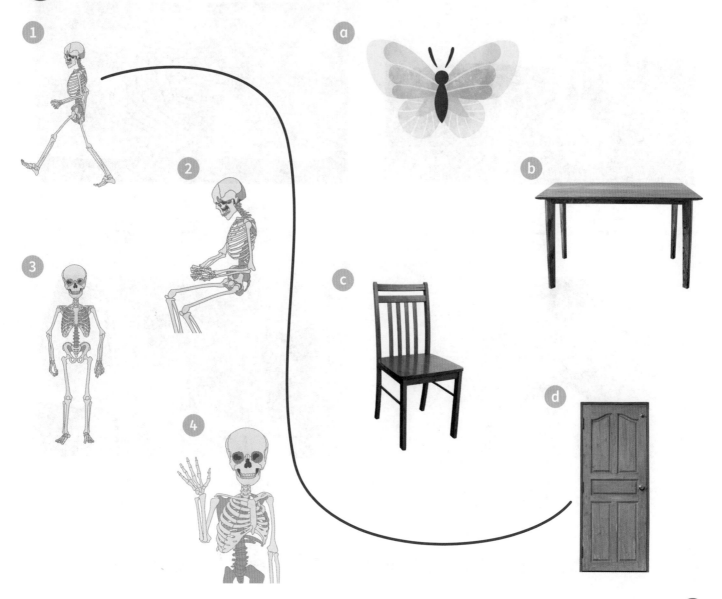

1 🎧28 **Listen and color.**

2 **Look at the pictures again. Circle a face for you.**

1  Look and say. Circle 😊, 😐, or 😞. **BIG QUESTION** How do we move?

2 Draw your favorite monster.

3 My Family

1 🎧 29 **Listen and color.**

mom

dad

sister

brother

grandpa

grandma

2 **Look and match. Say.**

1 🎧 30 **Listen and circle.**

2 🛡 **Draw someone from your family. Circle.**

This is my ...

mom   dad   brother   sister   grandpa   grandma

1 🎧 31 **Listen. Write numbers.**

mom	4
dad	☐
grandpa	☐
grandma	☐

2 🛡 **Draw your family.**

1 🎧 32 Listen. Circle ☑ or ☒.

1

☑ ⊗

2

☑ ☒

3

☑ ☒

4

☑ ☒

5

☑ ☒

6

☑ ☒

1 🎧 33 Listen and match.

2 Look and match.

1 What's good? Draw 😊.

2 Look at the family activities. Write 1, 2, and 3.

1 **Listen and color.**

chicken

dog

duck

cat

2 **Draw lines to make families.**

3 🎧35 Listen and draw.

4 Look and find your favorite family. Draw 😊.

1  **Listen and color. Say.**

2 **Look at the pictures again. Circle 😊, 😐, or 😟.**

1 Look and say. Circle 😊, 😐, or 😟.

2 Complete the family and color. Say.

BIG QUESTION What's a family?

4 At the Zoo

1 🎧 37 **Listen and number. Say.**

2 🛡 **Look and draw. Say.**

1

2

3

1 🎧38 Listen and check ☑.

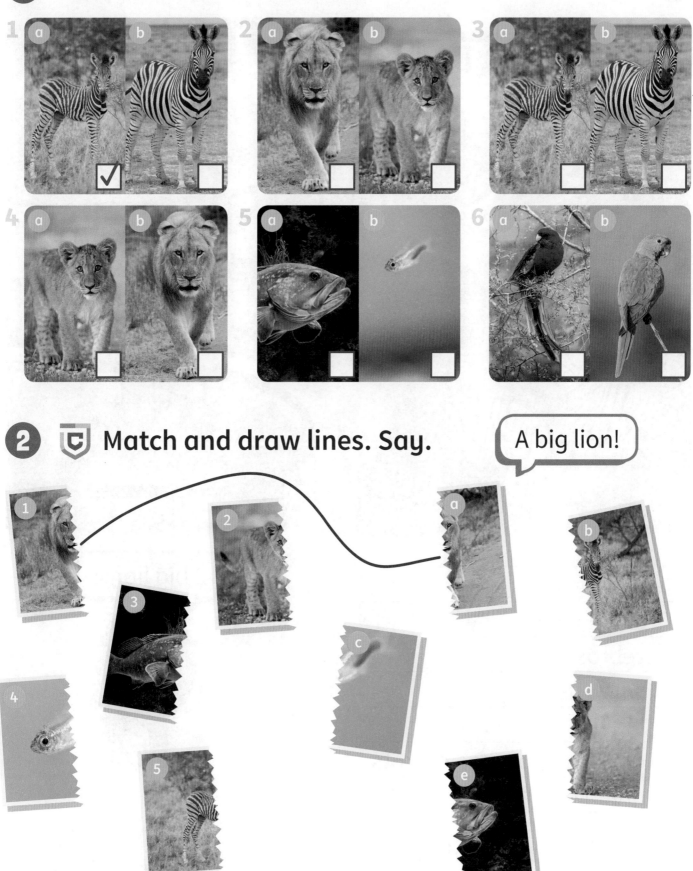

2 🛡 Match and draw lines. Say.

A big lion!

1 **Look. Count and write numbers. Say.**

2	big lions
	small lions
	zebras
	small fish
	big fish
	green and orange parrots
	green and red parrots

2 big lions!

2   **Listen and point.**

1 🎧40 Listen and check ☑.

2 🎧41 Listen and circle. Ask and answer.

① What's your favorite color?

It's red!

② What's your favorite number?

It's 6!

1 🎧42 Listen and number.

1

2 🎧43 Listen and check ☑.

1

2

1 What's good? Draw 😊.

2 Look at the friends. Write 1, 2, and 3.

1 **Listen and color. Say.**

monkey

frog

tree

pond

grassland

2 **Where do the animals live? Match and say.**

The monkey lives in the tree.

1

2

3

a

b

c

3 Look and circle the wrong animal.

4 Choose your favorite place. Draw 😊.

1 🎧 45 **Listen and number. Say.**

1

2 🛡 **Draw a picture of your favorite animal.**

My favorite animal is ...

1 Look and say. Circle , , or .

2 Where do they live? Look and check ✓.

 BIG QUESTION Where can we find animals?

3 Look and think. Draw animals in the pictures.

5 My Food

1 Match and say.

1 cupcakes
2 milk
3 chocolate
4 pears
5 oranges
6 tomatoes

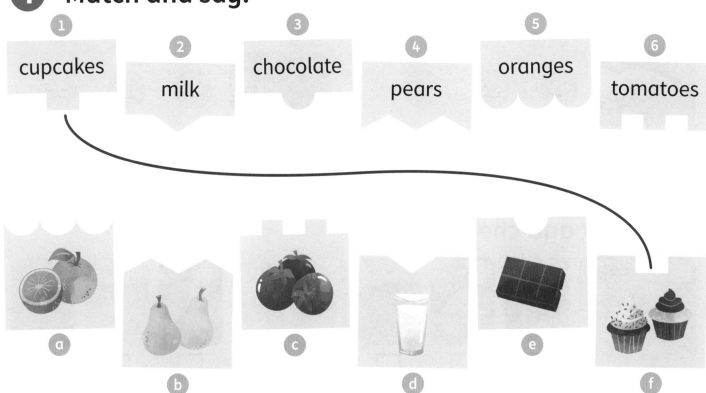

a
b
c
d
e
f

2 Look and count. Say.

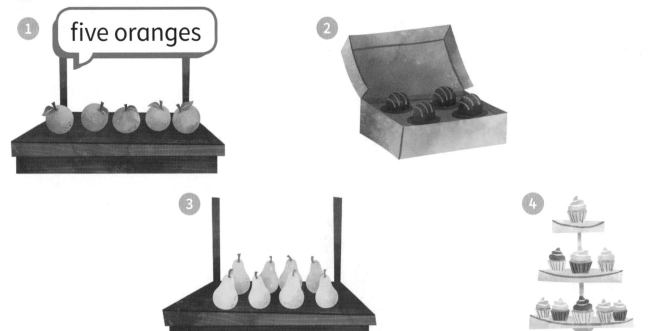

1 five oranges
2
3
4

1 🎧 46 **Listen and check ☑ or X ☒.**

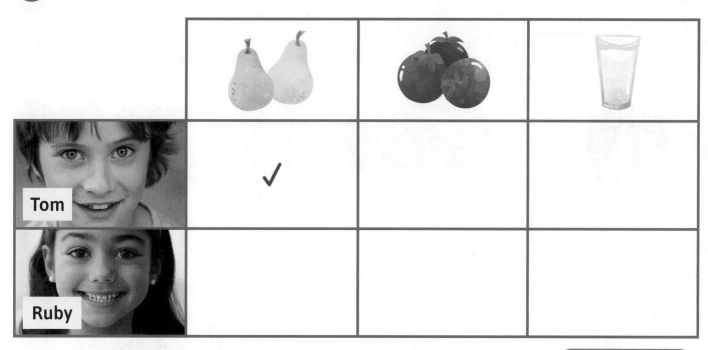

	🍐🍐	🍅🍅	🥛
Tom	✓		
Ruby			

2 🛡 **Circle 😊 or 😞 for you. Say.**

> I like tomatoes.

①

②

③

④

⑤

⑥

1 🎧 47 What do they like? Listen and circle.

1 I like ...   a b c

2 I like ...   a b c

2 Color, trace, and say.

I like you!

1 🎧 48 Listen and write *yes* or *no*.

1

y̶e̶s̶ / no

2

yes / no

3

yes / no

4

yes / no

5

yes / no

6

yes / no

2 Look and ask.

Do you like cake?

Yes, I do.

1 Follow the lines. Check ☑ or X ⊠.

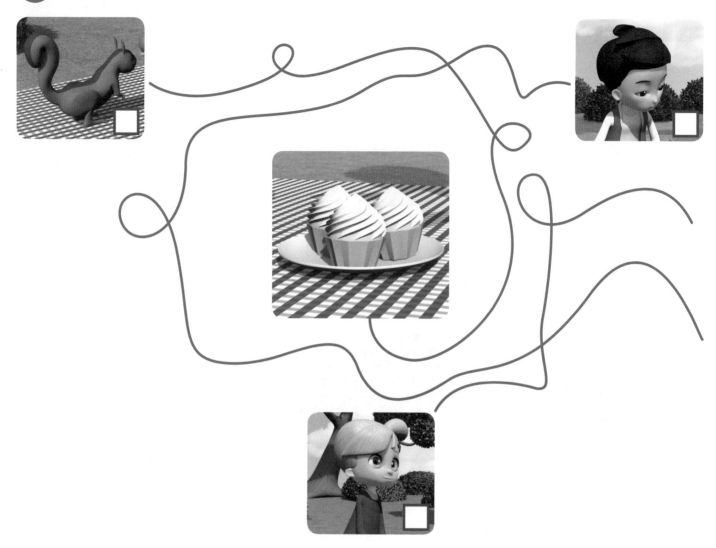

2 🛡 What's different? Look and say.

1 pear

1 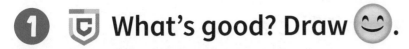 What's good? Draw 😊.

2 Complete the picture. Draw what a good friend does.

1 🛡 Which one is different? Circle.

1

a
b
c

2

a
b
c

3

a
b
c

2 🛡 Where does it come from? Trace and check ✓.

1
apple

2
orange

3
potato

4 banana

5
pear

6
carrot

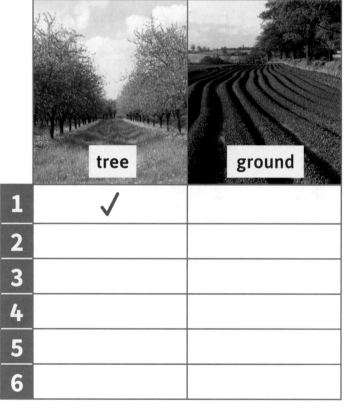

	tree	ground
1	✓	
2		
3		
4		
5		
6		

3 How many? Write.

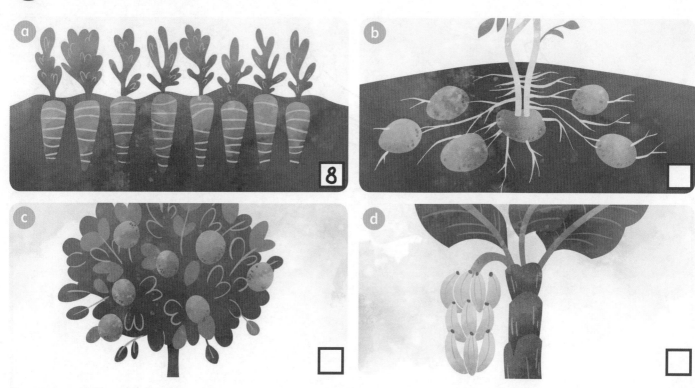

a | **8**

b | ☐

c | ☐

d | ☐

4 🛡 Draw the fruit. Trace.

My _____fruit_____ tree.

1  Make a "Super Fruit."

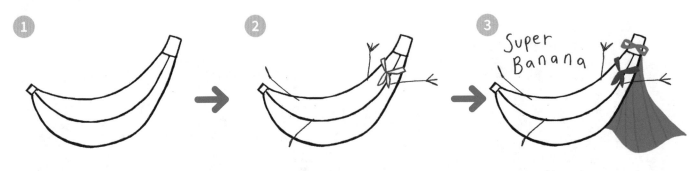

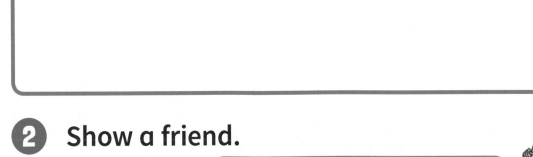

2 Show a friend.

Look, it's Super Banana!

1 Look and say. Circle 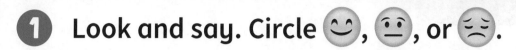, , or .

1

2

3

4

2 Tree or ground? Circle.

1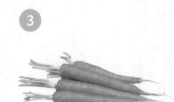

2

3

4

tree / ground   tree / ground   tree / ground   tree / ground

3 Choose and draw your picture.

 **BIG QUESTION** What food do we eat?

My favorite vegetable.

1 🎧 49 Listen and number.

2 Point and say.

Bus stop

1 🎧50 Listen and color.

Ava

Bob

Mia

Nick

2 Look at the maps. Point and say.

There's a toy store.

1   **Listen. What can you remember? Draw.**

2 **Look and write.**

park

hospital

store

1 Look and number.

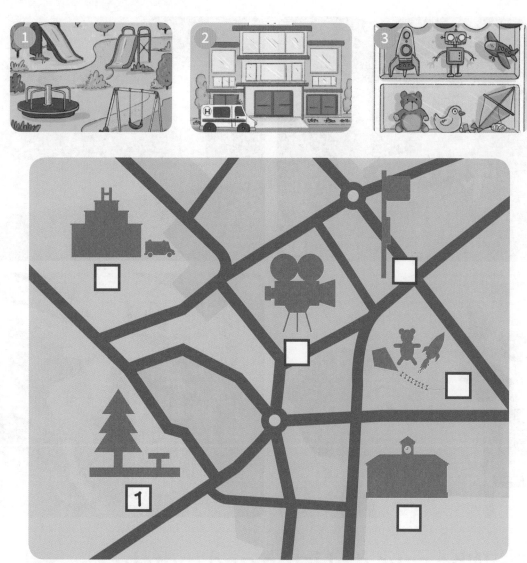

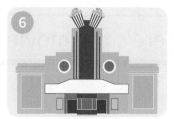

2 Look at the map. Ask and answer.

Where's the school?

It's there.

1 🎧52 Listen and number.

1

2 🎧53 Who says it? Listen and match.

1 There's the movie theater.

2 I have an idea!

3 Come with me.

1 What's good? Draw 😊.

2 Finish the picture. Draw what a good friend does.

1 Where are they? Look and say.

market

2 Look. Write and match.

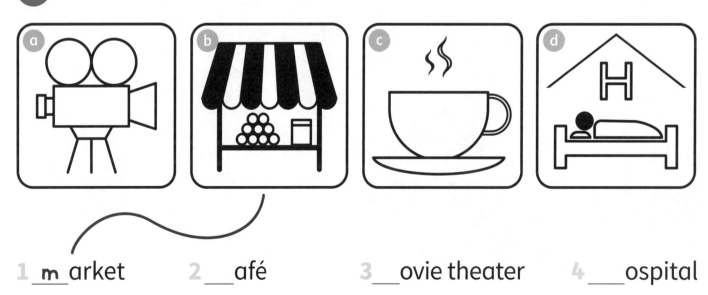

1 **m** arket   2 ___afé   3 ___ovie theater   4 ___ospital

3 🎧 **54** **Listen and draw a line. Start at X.**

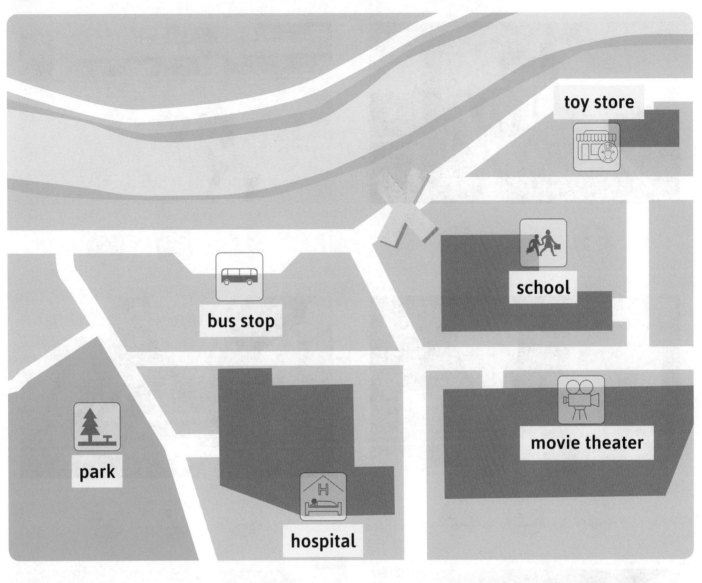

4 🛡 **Draw a place you know.**

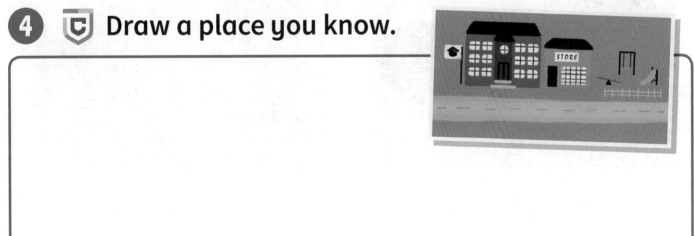

1 🎧55 Listen and color.

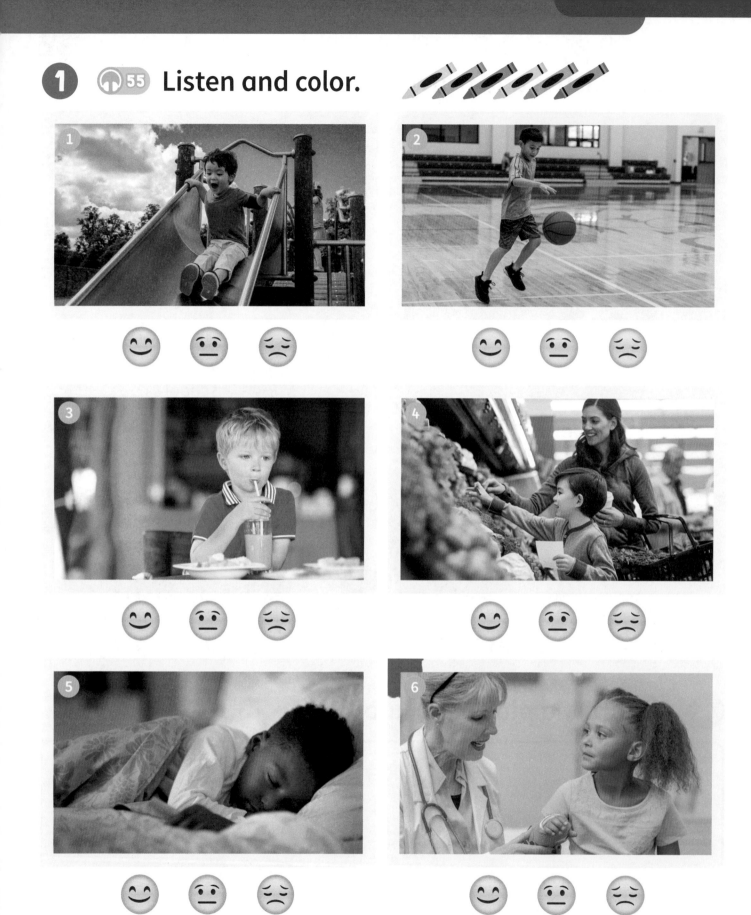

2 Look at the pictures again. Circle a face for you.

1 Look and say. Circle , , or .

2 What's in your town? Write *yes* or *no*.

BIG QUESTION — What's in your town?

yes / no _____ _____ _____

3 Draw a picture.

Me at my favorite place.

7 Jobs

1 Match and say.

firefighter

2 Look and write.

_t_ eacher

___et

___octor

___olice officer

___ardener

___irefighter

1 🎧56 **Listen. Write *yes* or *no*.**

_____yes_____

_____

_____

_____

_____

_____

2 **Look at the pictures again. Say.**

She's a police officer.

1 🎧57 Listen and trace.

2 Say "goodbye." Write.

good_____ _____ _____

1 🎧58 Look. Listen and check ☑.

1
a

b

2
a

b

3
a

b

2 Point and say.

He's a police officer.

1
2
3
4

5
6
7
8

9
10
11
12

Is he/she a (firefighter)? Yes, he/she is. No, he/she isn't.

1 **Who is it? Look and match.**

police officer   doctor   gardener

2 **Who wears it? Write *Whisper, Misty,* or *teacher*.**

teacher

_____

_____

_____

_____

_____

1 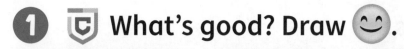 **What's good? Draw 😊.**

2 **Complete the picture.**

_____

Thank You

You are my best friend.

1 Write the first letters.

___armer

___entist

___alesclerk

2 🛡 Circle the correct words.

1 He is inside / outside.

2 She is inside / outside.

3 **Where are they? Look and say.**

He is outside.

4  **Trace and color.**

1 🛡 Make a job picture.

My Job Picture

2 Trace the title.

1 Look and say. Circle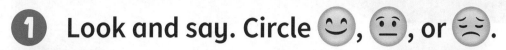

2 Inside or outside? Circle.

  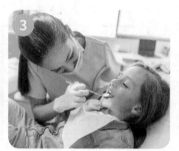 

inside / outside   inside / outside   inside / outside   inside / outside

3 Draw your favorite job.

 What's a job?

My favorite job

Review 79

1 Find the words.

n	c	o	a	t	e	l	a
k	j	e	a	n	s	h	w
g	d	s	c	a	r	f	m
s	w	e	a	t	e	r	f
j	t	g	l	o	v	e	s
t	s	h	i	r	t	b	i
q	b	o	o	t	s	u	v
s	o	c	r	p	h	a	t

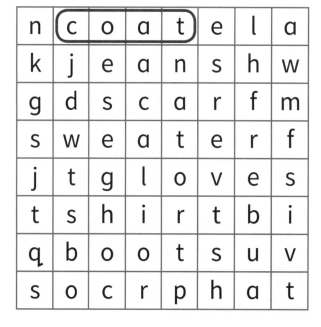

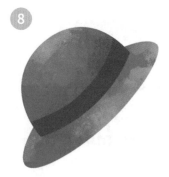

2 Look at pictures 1–8. Say.

sweater

1 🎧 **59** **Listen and draw.**

2 🛡 **Circle your clothes. Draw and say.**

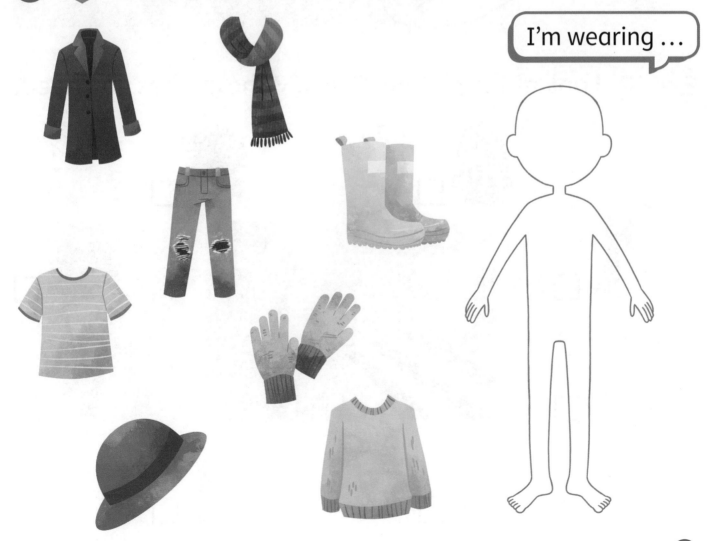

I'm wearing ...

1 🎧 60 What clothes do you need? Listen and circle.

2 🛡 Look at the picture. Check ☑ the clothes you need.

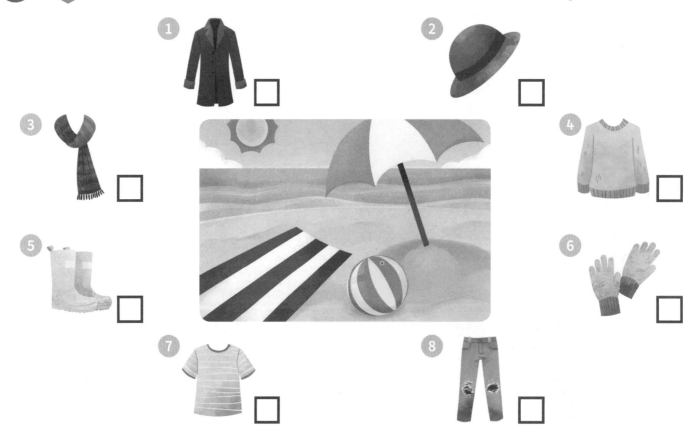

1 🎧 61 Listen. Write *yes* or *no*.

1 yes

2

3

4

5

6

2 Look at the pictures. Point and ask.

> Is he wearing a scarf?

> No, he isn't.

1 What's she wearing? Color and say.

2 🎧 62 Who says it? Listen and check ☑.

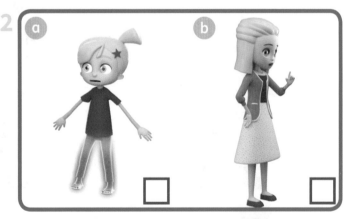
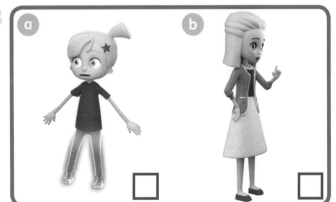
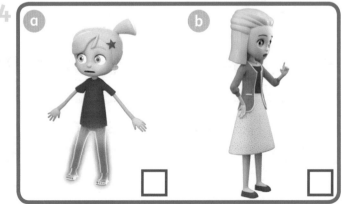

8

1  What's good? Draw 😊.

2 Trace the answer.

It's cold. Put a sweater on.

OK, Mom.

Value: Being Prepared 85

1 Complete the words. Match.

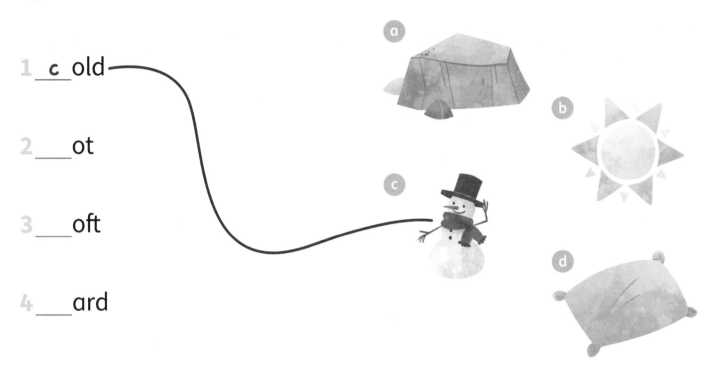

1 __c_ old

2 ___ot

3 ___oft

4 ___ard

a

b

c

d

2 Write *soft* or *hard*.

1 soft / hard

2 soft / hard

3 soft / hard

4 soft / hard

5 soft / hard

6 soft / hard

3 🛡 **Complete the words. Draw lines and match.**

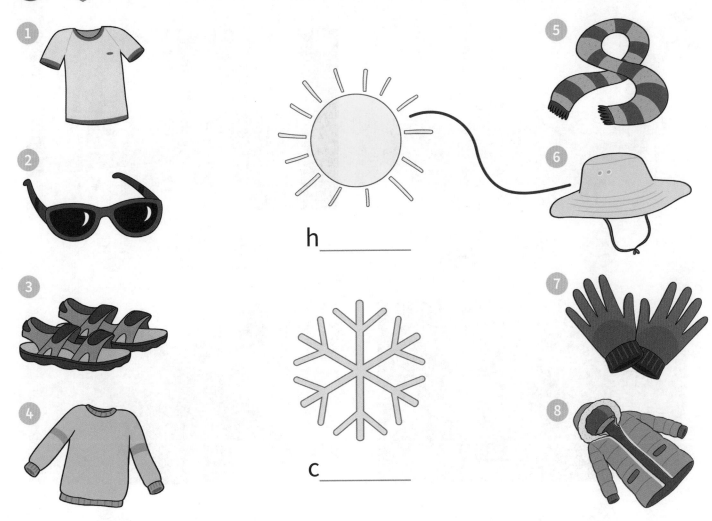

h_____

c_____

4 🛡 **Complete the picture. Trace.**

Me on a __cold__ day

2 **Look at the pictures again. Circle a face for you.**

1 Look and say. Circle , , or .

2 Hard or soft? Circle.

hard / soft   hard / soft   hard / soft   hard / soft

3 Finish the picture.

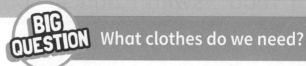 BIG QUESTION What clothes do we need?

My favorite _T-shirt_.

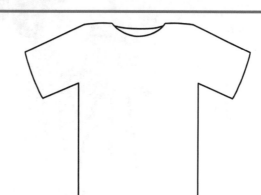

9 My Hobbies

1 Circle the hobby.

read / swim   paint / dance   run / play soccer

2 Look at the pictures. Write the words.

| read   swim   dance   paint a picture   play soccer   run |

_____   _____   _____

1 **Draw lines.**

I'm playing soccer.

I'm running.

I'm reading.

I'm dancing.

I'm swimming.

I'm painting a picture.

2 **Draw yourself and write.**

Look! I'm _____.

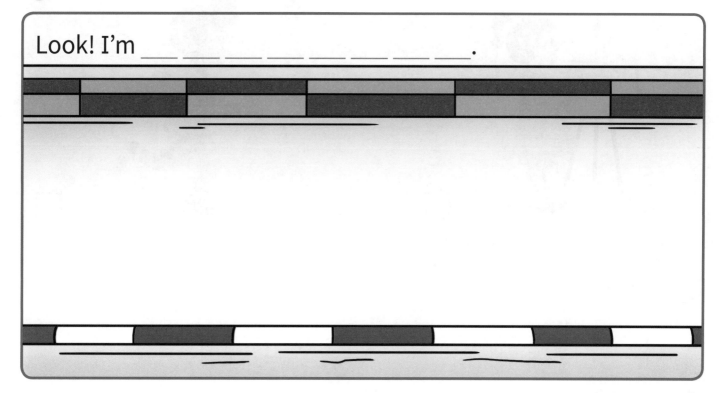

1 🎧 **64** **Listen and number 1–6.**

2 **Trace.**

Play today. I'm having fun.

1 🎧 65 **Listen. Write *yes* or *no*.**

yes _____ _____

_____ _____ _____

2 **Look at the photos. Write.**

Are you _____ _____?

Yes, I am.

Are _____ dancing?

_____, I'm _____.

1 🎧 66 Listen and number.

2 🎧 67 Who says it? Listen and check ☑.

1 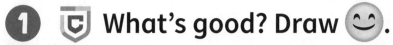 What's good? Draw 😊.

2 Write.

S _____

1 **Color the bars.**

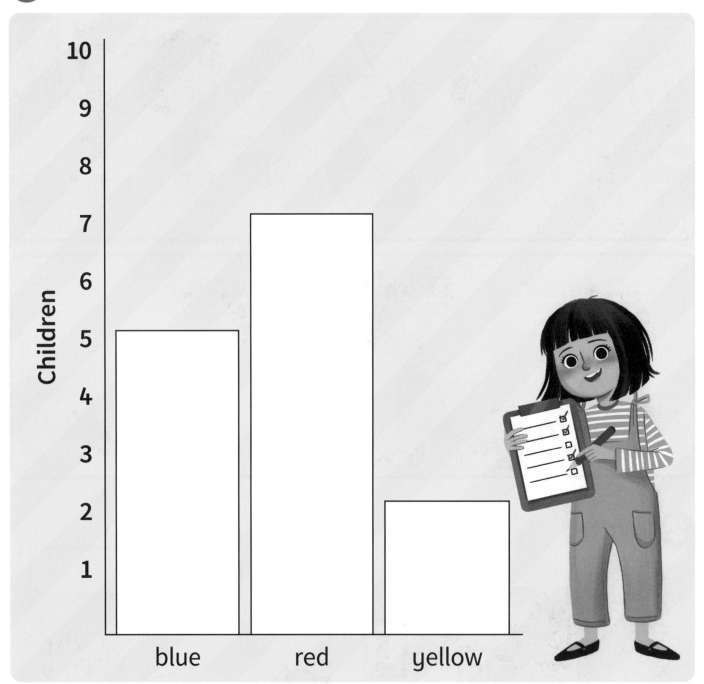

2 **Count. Complete the sentences.**

1 _____ children like blue.

2 _____ children like red.

3 _____ children like yellow.

3 Count and complete the tally chart.

Do you like ...?	
apples	
bananas	
oranges	

4 🛡 Draw the bar chart.

bananas

1

10

1 🛡 Make a guessing game.

1

2

What is he doing?

1 Look and say. Circle , , or .

2 Match the numbers and pictures.

Dancing	卌II
Reading	III
Playing Soccer	卌
Swimming	I

1 5 7 3

3 Draw your favorite hobby.

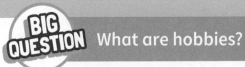
BIG QUESTION What are hobbies?

My favorite hobby

The Alphabet

1 Trace the letters.

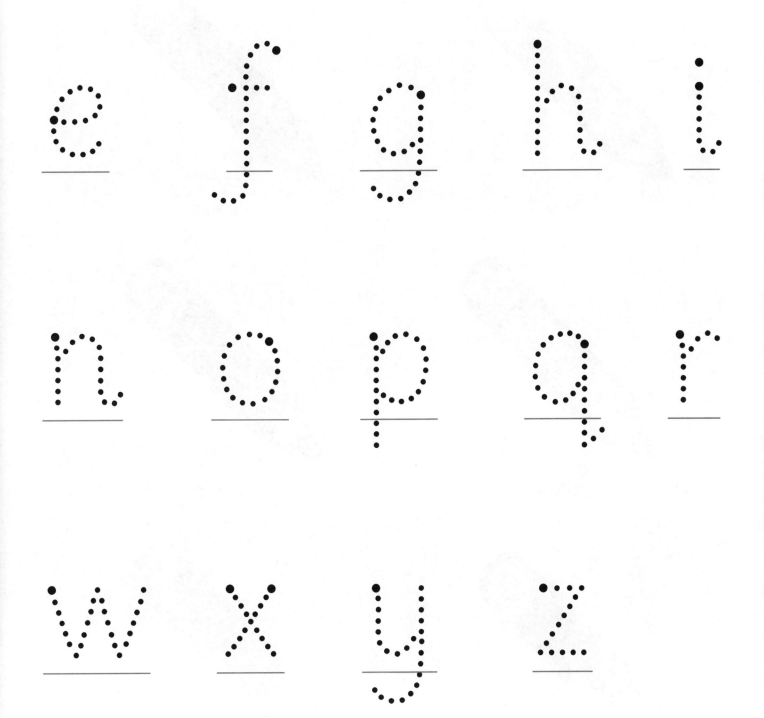

e f g h i

n o p q r

w x y z

Say Hello!

blue

green

yellow

orange

red

pink

one

two

three

four

five

six

seven

eight

nine

ten

window

book

table

door

pencil

chair

2 My Body

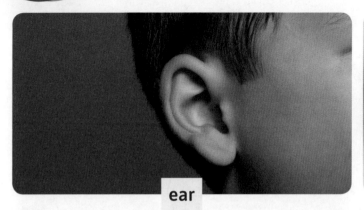

ear

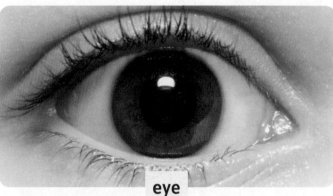

eye

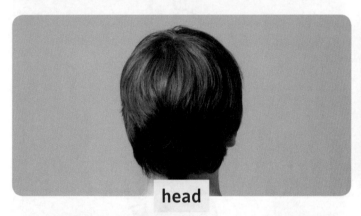

head

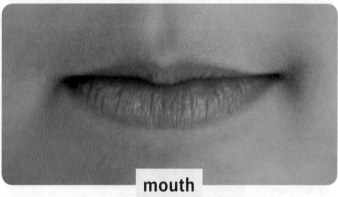

mouth

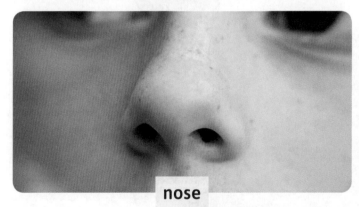

nose

arms

legs

3 My Family

grandma

brother

sister

grandpa

dad

mom

4 At the Zoo

fish

lion

monkey

parrot

zebra

frog

5 My Food

oranges

pears

tomatoes

milk

chocolate

cupcake

school

toy store

movie theater

bus stop

hospital

park

teacher

police officer

doctor

vet

firefighter

gardener

8 My Clothes

___oat

___eans

___carf

___loves

___oots

___-shirt

___at

___weater

9 My Hobbies

dance   paint   play soccer   read   run   swim

_____

_____

_____

_____

_____

_____